Flight

Also by Robert Anthony Gibbons

You Almost Home, Boy
Brooklyn, NY: Harlequin Creature, 2019

Close to the Tree: Poems
New York City: Three Rooms Press, 2012

Flight

Robert Anthony Gibbons

POETS WEAR PRADA • Hoboken, New Jersey

Flight

Copyright © 2019 Robert Anthony Gibbons

All rights reserved. Except for use in any review or for educational purposes, the reproduction or utilization of this work in whole or in part in any form by electronic, mechanical or other means, now known or hereafter invented, including xerography, photocopying and recording, or in any informational or retrieval system, is forbidden without the written permission of the publisher:

Poets Wear Prada
533 Bloomfield Street, Second Floor
Hoboken, New Jersey 07030
http://pwpbooks.blogspot.com

First North American Publication 2019

Mass Market Paperback Edition 2019

ISBN-13: 978-1-946116-07-9
ISBN-10: 1-946116-07-6

Printed in the U.S.A.

Cover Art: Steve Dalachinsky
Author Photo: Ming Chan

For Robert Harris

Table of Contents

Flight: Ewig Weibliche / Eternal Feminine	3
Flight: North Dakota	4
Flight: Wisconsin	5
Flight: Minnesota	6
Flight: Hays, Kansas	7
Flight: #94	8
Flight: Helena	9
Flight: Montana	10
Flight: Sweet Pea	11
Flight: Snow	12
Flight: Alphabet City, Oregon, 2013	13
Flight: Antioch, Tennessee	14
Flight: A Sestina Found on the Pacific Coast	15
Flight: Datebook via Pacifica	17
Flight: Zuma Beach	18
Flight: Southern New Jersey	19
Flight: Andrada	20
About the Author	23
About the Cover Artist	24

Flight

Flight

Flight: Ewig Weibliche / Eternal Feminine

I am over Lake Superior with Robert,
Looking down on the crystalline blue.
Something else, too:
There's a woman next to him.

She takes a tissue from her purse, and
Begins to cry. She sweats like a pot in

The boiling heat. Robert takes her hands;
And she holds his. The schoolchildren

Across the aisle watch the scene:
Fingers get in between fingers.

We wait for clearance and the voice of
The captain. Open up the shades to

The glare. The unbearable chest
Of Earth. The shoreline traces the lake.

I want to see God's vision:
Creation from this distance.

Flight: North Dakota

I am cold, pulled from a deep freeze,
and asked to thaw, your Winnipeg night,
near your border. It is always partly
cloudy but fair. I fly over, past Grand Forks
and Bismarck. I want to know the local
time of origin.

Can't decide how to divide you,
with the basket as low as Nebraska.
Call you Sioux, then fall for you.

Flight: Wisconsin

I can't decide. There is smoke.
A thousand windows, too.
Fantasy. No land, just
Storms.

The color, sand, and want
Fall into the neck and nape.
Check for the sex in others.

You are teasing. I call from behind
The skirt of clouds. I want the chance
To be young while it's fun
And routine.

Not be the manual to find you. Point
Down is where you will find me.
I will be stone and Borglum rock.

Nature has its consequences.
Your friendly exposures bowl me over.
I hide, then return for the ride.

Flight: Minnesota

It is bumpy on this side of the country,
Now that Robert and I are past the
Mississippi.

The hip-hop of his fingertips —
And I am naked as a cloud shrouded
Down on this lake.

The face parcels off for miles.
There are long roads in Upper
Sioux land, and

Mandans and buffalos, so I will
Take it slow, discover the forest,
Get lost in the witness.

Three more states of consciousness.
Another stratosphere to plow.
I am in it. I want to conquer.

If it takes time zones or honing
In on dialect, I will try it all
For effect.

Flight: Hays, Kansas

I should call you Geraldine or Winifred;
Instead I am in a haze. The smoke blazes into
Infinity. Looks eternal. Choked,

I gloat each secret, each moment
As it gets thicker, this deliverer of clouds,
Down near the wide mouth of the river.

Heaven may be white — with steeple, plain and
Simple — only clouds for miles; death and
Resurrection preface the stars.

Nothing but the eternal feminine.

Flight: #94

I thought of a river,
But it could be a road —

A connected menage à quatre:
Regina to Helena,

Billings to Calgary. There
Are three in bedrock,

Mistakes in ownership. All
I want is exterior,

The untamed outside. Reminds
Me of fish nets and high hills

All the way to Anita. Sure
I will please you. Caught

In your big horns.

Flight: Helena

What are all these undulations with Grandmother?
Spider skillets or varicose, cracks open like turnips,

Simmers in the middle of the pot. Then we put them
To boil. I could be spoiled by this land. Could settle

On a parcel. Will call you Angela or Jordan. Would
Call you Broadway. All the feminine anniversaries.

Want to reap years of field work. I will till for you.
Bring me through the winter. Through this bitter

Distance. I have traveled for you.

Flight: Montana

It gets more defined as I trace the lines.
The clouds are smoke screens to Rapid

City. I want my own GPS to track
Distance. We are approaching Billings,

But Robert calls her Isabel with the
Estimated time of arrival. Landlocked, she gives off

Hot flashes as we close in on the Rockies,
As we move around her block.

Buffalo and bison leave a trail of dust.
She is big country. *If I could have my run*

Of you, it would be a great fall, with atmosphere
And heaven near. Only one minute before

We hit her border, then taste her shoulder
Of road. *Keep me, warm mountain*

and bland sky, sun dance on the plain!

Flight: Sweet Pea

Traveled a black road, a trail
Physical and emotional, to the corner

Of Powell Street with a fat porch, moss
hanging across its rails. There are turnips,

Watermelons, small orbs which sit in red clay;
Yellow pears spill over the rusted gate.

Lima and butter beans made us go
Down a winding road, potbelly

Stomachs full of apple butter and tomato,
En route to Sweet Pea.

Flight: Snow

This time there are card games,
Secrets as old as the chifferobes,

Allowances made in the front room
For pee-pots and spittoons, dollies

And antique brooms used to sweep, daily.
The ritual: to totter — it seems pitiful.

But just around the kitchen,
I hear the snow.

Flight: Alphabet City, Oregon, 2013

I met Lula in Alphabet City, Oregon.
In lilywhite and hydrangea, where
streets are categorized in Williams-
burg palettes, where big bay windows
color the Willamette River.

She groped me over quiche and
buckwheat, over asparagus for
breakfast, goblets of port and
homemade cookies, silver platters,
ornate moldings, bed frames, duvets
with five hundred pieces of thread.

She locked me in the dressing parlor
with a rocking chair, with magazines on
antiquity, and it was the dead of winter,
then the middle of the summer. I could
hear the roar of kayaks, pantries and
closets with a bivouac of emotion.

Her eyes followed me down the cobble-
stones to the bottom of the hill, to
Everett and Savior. She had no idea
I was from a place of dichotomy,
juxtaposed autonomy.

Flight: Antioch, Tennessee

You may call it prayer because my mother is here,
but the roads are slick and lonely with the bare cold
as we roll down this neighborhood. There are no birds
just earthworms to sizzle on fresh concrete, in the bottom
of a skillet as I search for verse in this overworked
ground full of dull-yellow and black-bottom brown
people who mind their business, and I guess I should
leave the rest to history. And the news of the day is
it's snowing in Memphis, so there is no reason to be
restless, so I am still blessed with the family in the
monogamy of blood. And they have come here for the first
time. For a holiday. For the solitary function to be together.
And I thought I would not enjoy Central Time, but I want
Florida like the dragonfly wants the migration down South.
But the word of mouth, for a few more days in the old
year, just a few more days for salvation: we can be saved —
not by church or synagogue but by the dialogue of nephews
and nieces, and pieces of potato pie and giblets of collard
greens made with love and the stove which still steams in
my background. And I will leave in a few days in the old
year, anew with a few more memories, will leave the old
year behind. I can find my way back through the
calendar. And it will be the rush of trucks, the run of the
expressway. This is enough to frame my thought, enough
to say I have gained memory — only a moment.

Flight: A Sestina Found on the Pacific Coast

It's only an hour until I board. I want to get there,
to the other end, to make Pacific time. There it is
above me, my longitude and latitude packed,
my bags. I am tagged like a tat as I sit
between unknown people — some too big —
because I want the Tacoma sun.

I want the red of mestizo brick, the pinpricked sun
of Sitka spruce, and to follow the river there
when I touch down on Walla-Walla, big
corner of the universe. A burst that is
fog and lighthouse not smog that sits
as in skyscraper but tapers the evergreens packed

while salmon snake upriver, packed
with the Wishram man and his papoose. The sun
makes me lose my nativism as I sit
like a caboose. Want to see oddities there,
antiquities as bleak as the forest is,
pick cherries in the Draper Valley. Big

bold women ride yellow bicycles, big
gourmet trucks. Makes me not rush. Not a packed
subway train but the smell of rain is
there in the state of Oregon, in Sun-

river when I touch down on Walla-Walla. There
is Georgia O'Keefe to follow; cow skulls sit

from 1933. I want to be as old as gold, sit
like tumbleweed, the colors of Mardi Gras, big
as Lincoln's Oregon oak. Want to find N.C. Wyeth there,
and Robert Colescott, when I touch down, packed
with kayak on the Willamette River. Forage me sun
when I commune with the octopus tree as sacred as time is.

Convince me that to be transcontinental is
to be as traveled as the railroad — sit
carpetbagger, a swagger of tonic. The sun
is fresh air, the God-given big
nests of earth freshly packed,
my moon river. Finally made it there.

Yes, I finally made it there. She's a big
country! To sit veranda style, take in air, sun
while hydrangeas wrap is all I need. Bags, now, unpacked.

Flight: Datebook via Pacifica

It is an enormous phenomenon to entertain nature,
to hear a coyote devour a deer, the grunt and gruel
of a mountain lion, when the sounds frighten,

the heightened howls not contained in the city.
The toxic flora and succulent fauna. The weather-
exposed remains of a carcass that appear to be a skull,
near the parking lot.

Its fangs, relics for the museum cabinet. By the jagged
rough-hewn rock that juts out like archipelago. We stir
with the wind, with the bright perfumery of eucalyptus
and wild lavender. Scatter like the ivy.

Yes, the hills are alive. Not a cow skull of Georgia O'Keefe's
but some weather-exposed skeleton was left — as witness.

Flight: Zuma Beach

It's so hot, think
I'll bake myself
into chocolate,
will sea salt soap;

almond butter
will become sunscreen
between sky
and sea;

without urge
or plea, my toes
will row boats —
as motes

back to God,
back to eternity;
I'll bake
into chocolate —

the sand,
a riot
of delicious grease.

Flight: Southern New Jersey

Went to visit a sick relative. Had to take a bus — don't remember which one — down the center of the state. For the bus served as a local and state service. At the bus depot, lives are in and out. I kept my biggie coat close for protection from the winter chill. As we crossed the Maurice River, it was so spoken word. This is the land of big shopping malls and urban sprawl. The trees have no facial degeneration. They don't suffer from smoke stacks or chemicals, but the roads are wide and vacant. Dotted with parking lots and shoppers. Super, rotisserie, deli, and ATM.

It was faraway but close. The streets had names like Liberty and Maple, Boxwood and Captain. I could never live there. If they expect me to buy a flatbed truck to carry dog food, big packages are out of the question. Pulling up to a gas station and saying "fill her up" is not in my vocal range, but I understand the innocence.

Flight: Andrada

Tried to understand the reason
I commune with you. It's rather risky
to compromise the trope on a common New York statue.
If I had my choice, you would be Mnemosyne,
the goddess of memory. Or Lincoln, with his cloak
and cape. Picked through the garbage too, copped
a can at Union Square, but

I am where I am.
And who is Jose Silva
to bring me such a gift, if he is
the Patriarch of Brazilian Independence?

I sit here in silence.
Only the rhythms of the street sweeper,
only Whitman's "learn'd astronomer"
in this backdrop of a busy Bryant park,
playing ampersand and fellatio in three eight time.
Maybe you gave me the poem
in my pocket.

Andrada, in quiet reflection,
in juxtaposition with Lincoln.
your straightened coiffure and tuxedo
does not bother me.

Andrada, this Ellis Island harbor
receives you. Maybe you know
more than we give credit.
We pass by like
Oppen skyscrapers
looking down at you.

Andrada, in repetition,
your inhibitions are mine.
As singular and isolated.
Ostracized with polished patina.

Your uncompromising demeanor.
Just keep going, Andrada.
Just keep standing, Andrada.
There are no blinds among
the hedges, Andrada.

It's tough sitting on a stone bench,
looking for a lonely fix, Andrada.
There are only fifteen minutes,
Andrada, to give me just
what I need.

About the Author

Robert Anthony Gibbons, a native Floridian, came to New York City in 2007 in search of his muse Langston Hughes and found a vibrant contemporary poetry community at the Cornelia Street Cafe, the Green Pavilion, Nomad's Choir, Brownstone Poets, Hydrogen Jukebox, Saturn Series, and Phoenix among other venues. His first book, *Close to the Tree*, was published by the New York-based Three Rooms Press in 2012.

Robert currently works as a Literature Professor at the City College of New York. He is a Cave Canem Fellow (2019-2021) and has received residencies from the Norman Mailer Foundation (2017) and the DISQUIET International Literary Program (2018). In 2018 he completed his MFA at City College.

He has been published in over thirty literary magazines and in several notable anthologies. Recent publication credits include *Expound*, *Promethean*, *Turtle Island Quarterly*, *Killer Whale*, and *Suisun Valley Review*, and the forthcoming *Bronx Memoir Project: Vol. 2*, published by the Bronx Council of the Arts.

Robert lives in Brooklyn and continues to be active in the New York poetry scene. *Flight* is his third poetry collection.

About the Cover Artist

Brooklyn-born poet and collage artist Steve Dalachinsky is a 2014 recipient of a Chevalier de l'Ordre des Arts et des Lettres. His books include the PEN Oakland National Book winner *The Final Nite* (Ugly Duckling Press, 2006) and his most recent collection, *Where Night and Day Become One: The French Poems* (Great Weather for Media, 2018), which won an IBPA Benjamin Franklin Award. His latest CD is *Pretty in the Morning* with the French rock group The Snobs (Bisou Records, 2019).

About the Photographer

Ming Chan is a New York-based photographer who pursues the romantic ideals of the human spirit. His works span genres — portrait, landscape, event, and street photography — and reflect his sincere desire to craft images that speak to our communal self. You can follow his work on Flickr where he goes by MKC609.

A NOTE ABOUT THE TYPE

Beatrice Warde (1900–1969), typography scholar and educator, author of the classic *The Crystal Goblet* (World, 1956), a collection of 16 essays on the subject of book typography, often said the reader's eye should focus "*through* type and not *upon* it." In an address delivered to British Typographers Guild, Warde compared type to a window "between the reader inside the room and that landscape which is the author's work." Ornate type like a stained-glass window, however admired, Warde warned, cannot provide a clear view of that landscape, and in fact obscures it. For Warde the beauty of type was not to be found in flourishes & curves, metered stress of slants & horizontals or in calculated geometric proportions but rather in their inconspicuousness. The subdued elegance of Verdana, sans serif except to distinguish characters, designed specifically for legibility—on the computer screen (that literal glass now virtually ubiquitous between the reader and world), yet pleasing on the printed page, would have charmed Ms. Warde.

Verdana was commissioned by Microsoft Corporation in the 1990s and developed by British type designer Matthew Carter. Before Carter designed Verdana for Microsoft in 1993, most computer typefaces had been adapted from traditional metal-set print type, often resulting in letters that appeared scrawny and pathetic (especially italics) on the low-resolution screens of the period. Virginia Howlett, then a member of Microsoft's typography team, recognized the demand for legible screen fonts and the prevailing popularity of contemporary sans-serif typefaces used in advertising like Helvetica and Univers. Matthew Carter was commissioned to collaborate on what remains to this day to be one of the most prevalent and popular of all computer fonts.

Dubbed "the most widely read man" (*The New Yorker*, 2005) for the volumes of text rendered in his still ever so popular type fonts (Verdana, Georgia, Tahoma, etc.), Carter has designed fonts for *Le Monde*, *The New York Times*, *Time*, *The Washington Post*, *The Boston Globe*, *Wired*, *Newsweek*, and *Sports Illustrated*, as well as Bell Centennial (commissioned by AT&T) for the phone book. In addition to commissions, his typography has earned him worldwide recognition and several awards including a MacArthur "genius grant" (2010). Seven of Carter's typefaces including

Verdana are in the permanent collection of the Museum of Modern Art, where they were displayed in MoMA's *Standard Deviations* exhibition (2011-12).

In 2009, the world's largest furniture retailer IKEA, famous for its savvy-marketing of design to the masses, caused a furor in the design and advertising communities by going *digital*—abandoning New Frankfurt's Futura to adopt Microsoft's Verdana for the design store's catalog typeface. While spokespeople for IKEA explained the change as a necessary step to unify branding between print and web media (Futura still proprietary and Verdana a widely distributed system font), critics were outraged that a typeface designed by Silicon Valley, specifically for the web, would supplant one by Werkbund, for books and as art, by appearing in print in the nearly 200 million catalogs distributed worldwide annually. However, the customers never complained.

Verdana was Brant Lyon's choice for his—and Poets Wear Prada's—debut collection, *Your Infidel Eyes*, released in 2006. He said he wanted a sans-serif font, but no "geeky" Arial, nothing as "slick" as Helvetica, something more "humanist." He may have been secretly anticipating a future e-book, but his choice works quite well on paper. Like Lyon's writing, Verdana never obscures the landscape, and its calligraphic style well suits the human inhabitants.

Before Lyon died in 2012, he co-founded two other poetry houses, UpHook Press and great weather for MEDIA. He also established his own spoken word recording label, Logo Chrysalis Productions. These promotional activities in addition to hosting the Hydrogen Jukebox POEMusic series had a significant impact on the careers of many emerging poets. One of the newcomers Lyon met and subsequently published and recorded was Robert Anthony Gibbons.

Gibbons's poetry can be heard on the CD *Brain Ampin'* (Logo Chrysalis Productions) and appears in the anthologies *hell strung and crooked* (UpHook Press) and *The Understanding between Foxes and Light* (great weather for MEDIA). *Flight* is our fifth travel-inspired book. Lyon's *Your Infidel Eyes* was our first, followed by Maria Lisella's *Two Naked Feet,* B.E. Kahn's *Landscapes of Light*, and Joel Allegretti's *Europa / Nippon / New York*. You may recognize the OCR-B font used on the book cover from Allegretti's book. OCR-B is also used worldwide for machine-readable passports as well as boarding passes. It was developed in 1968 by Adrian Frutiger for Monotype.

www.ingramcontent.com/pod-product-compliance
Lightning Source LLC
Chambersburg PA
CBHW071804040426
42446CB00012B/2700